BLOOD
FROM
ANGELS'
WINGS

BLOOD
FROM
ANGELS'
WINGS

BROTHER TOM

authorHOUSE®

AuthorHouse™ LLC
1663 Liberty Drive
Bloomington, IN 47403
www.authorhouse.com
Phone: 1-800-839-8640

Published by AuthorHouse   09/21/2013

ISBN: 978-1-4184-4732-8 (sc)
ISBN: 978-1-4184-6615-2 (e)

Any people depicted in stock imagery provided by Thinkstock are models, and such images are being used for illustrative purposes only.
Certain stock imagery © Thinkstock.

This book is printed on acid-free paper.

CONTENTS

Illustration Credits

<u>Cover</u>

Bearer of Good Tidings
by Amy Guip

The Gift
by Thomas Paonessa
model: Connie Bederka

The Fifth Station
by Thomas Paonessa

Broken Clock – Public Domain
(file name: broken clock)

The Rose
by Alexander Young

The Warrior King
by Mike Winterheimer
Model: Tom Paonessa

Cigarettes for Breakfast?
by Thomas Paonessa

Prayer and Meditation
by Albrecht Durer

Broken Eggs
by Thomas Paonessa

Family Portrait
by Dr. Mary W. Paonessa

Jesus Walking on Water
by Thomas Paonessa

As it is noted in the original certificate registration, the poems "Angel's Tears" and "A Warrior King's Soliloquy" have derivative influence from the work, "Atlantic Night Trip" by Christopher Collins.

The poem "DASH" uses the expression "Watcha gonna do with your dash?", commonly used by extreme sports fanatics.

The poem P.S.A. 0.0 has derivative influence from the song, "Tourniquet," by Evanescence.

An Invitation

I asked God to be with me tonight,
    as I read my poetry.

He politely declined.

So, I'll be doing this solo tonight.

I hope you don't mind.

But if I can touch just one person tonight,
maybe then there he shall be.

For the union of two
provides a warmer hearth
than the neediness of merely one.

And *that* would make a proper invitation.

Yes, maybe he'll show up tonight.

Dedication

I hope that the words in this book will best represent who I am. Maybe then I can read it over and discover myself. Whatever I find on these pages, I dedicate to my father, John J. Paonessa. I wish I could have told him how much he was loved and how greatly I was going to miss him.

The Gift

I was walking along the beach, looking for the Lord. I saw Him up ahead and, after I caught up to Him, I silently waited until He turned and noticed me.

I then approached Him and said, "Lord, I have something to offer You. Oh, it isn't much. It's dirty, it's grimy and it's filthy . . . but it's straight from the heart."

He took into His hands and examined it carefully . . . and said nothing. It was then I thought my gift was not worthy of His attentions. Feeling rejected, I turned to leave.

"Wait!" He said.

I turned once again and stared into His loving eyes. From the shining brilliance of the moonlight I saw a teardrop slowly roll down His cheek and stain into His beard.

"This is a gift that I have been waiting for all of My life." He said. "This is a part of you. I cannot ask of a gift greater than this.

"Because of your generous offer, we shall now be able to grow all the more closer. And you shall be able to grow closer to yourself. You are a good and worthy human being - it would be a shame if you never got to know you."

He then said that He had to leave. After reassuring me that I had never been and never will be alone, He walked up into his Father's House and waved to me.

I then walked back along the surf to share my story with others.

Poetry Canal

What kind of poetry do I wanna write?
I wanna write the kind of poetry
that you can't shake a stick at
but you can shake your ass to.

I wanna write the kind of poetry
that can sail you right up into the stars
but then drop you right back down in the dirt
and never let you forget you're clay and dust
and from whence you came and so shall you go.

I wanna be vulgar
and I wanna be elevated.
And I wanna be both

And I wanna be
        wanna be
                be right now.

And I tell ya'
when life takes that big ol' nail
        and rips it on down
into the palm of my hand
        and slams it on down onto a block of wood

I wanna be there writin' all about it.
Yeah,
I wanna write about pain like that
And I wanna write about the flesh and the blood
and the cartilage and the sinew

But I also wanna be able to write about my soul
and they may be rippin' my body apart
but my spirit's doin' just fine,
thank you.

There's a little boy who what tells me how much he likes blue
but that green is his favorite.

And you know how you've driven by that noisy ol' airport a hundred times and you don't
even hardly notice it no more, but then that little boy sees all them lights lit up and down
the runways

and his eyes pop open
and his mouth drops open
and he says, "pretty!"

Yeah, I wanna write about that too mama.

I wanna write about it all!

I want everything I see, feel, hear, and touch to come on down through my fingertips and teach them a lesson they won't never forget.

I wanna shake 'em on down to their roots, pummel 'em, and stroke 'em. And when they finally emerge from the filter of my sensibilities, it's almost like givin' birth.

And those words will be what they never thought they could be.

My heavens, how I love bein' a midhusband for The Word.

The Man on the Tree

Damn the man who died on the tree
and damn Him for loving me.

Damn Him for His example
and for expecting so much.

How can I love everyone else
when sometimes I can't even love myself?

(You don't have to love everyone else.
 Just let me love them - through you.
 Be my vessel.)

Wait!
Maybe the truth will come pouring into me
in a solemn and mighty rush
if I turn to Buddha instead.
in whispered words and hushed
tones he might tell me what he said
under the Bo tree.

And the beauty of Koans
will lead me home
and I'll be able to trace
back to - what?

Will enlightenment come to me
in a moment of Sartori?
And will a hundred one-armed monks applaud me for my efforts?

No. I don't think so. That's not my destiny.
I'll have to find something else for me.

But one thing I know for certain - and that is:
I will not die for the man who died for me.
He may have split the earth and ripped the curtain
but he expects too much of me.

(I would never expect anything of you
 that I have not done myself.)

Maybe drugs can be my answer instead.
Yeah.
Smoke a few doobs and pop a few reds.

Inject a dream into a vein
and all my problems will fade away.
No more garbage.
No more pain.

But sooner or later
there's always a price to pay.
When the fat lady has sung
and the piper has played.

Your fingertips start to bleed
and your nose starts to itch
as you're doin' coke
in a Texaco men's room.

No,
I have to break away from that scene
and go somewhere else

And I'm not sure where that's gonna be
but it's not gonna be
with the man on the tree.

Because I'm . . .

Because I'm . . .

scared.

(Why are you scared?)

I don't know.

(Why are you scared?)

I said I don't know!

(Why are you scared?)

Because I don't want to die! O.K.?!

I mean, I just don't want to die.

Only those who are born
and born again
truly are alive.
But you do not have the heart
to do this, because you
do not want to die.

I understand.

It is a very long journey from the mind to the heart.

But it begins with just one step.
Yet wonderfully, beautifully, it ends
with the very same step.

And if you take that one little baby miracle leap,
you will not be dashed upon the rocks below-No!
They will rise up to meet you on your way.

And then, hand in hand, side by side,
we can walk down that rocky garden path-together.

(I love the man who died on the tree.
And I love Him for saving me.)

War and Prayer

Holy Mary, mother of

my God
my God
Why have You abandoned me?

Bless me Father, for I have.

The blood flows
and the sand stains
But oil runs thicker than blood

Pray for us sinners

And where shall the Word be found
And where shall the Word resound?

Rachel weeps, uncomforted, for her children.

now until the hour of our death

Amen.

The Fifth Station

Pick up my cross and follow Me.

What? Do you think you are not worthy of the task
because you are just a man or just a woman?
Well, was not Simon just a man?

Sweet Simon of Cyrene-An unknown farmhand who helped Me in My hour of need and now, because of that chance encounter, his name has gone down through the ages. A simple act of kindness remembered throughout all eternity.

Nothing more is known of him.

Did he have a family?
Did he enjoy his work?
Was he a holy man?

It doesn't matter.

He picked up My cross and he followed Me.

That is all you need know.

Now, what will you do?

A sympathetic stranger lit a candle in the middle of the night and now a light shines for all the earth to see. Will you turn to that light so that you may in turn become a beacon for others and lead them to my eternal flame of salvation?

Or are you going to wallow in your own self-pity, lamenting over past hurts,
and crying over the injustices of the world?

Judean thorns and loyal friends
Crucifixions and rainbows
There's no beginning 'till there's an end
And no prayer as precious
as a broken prayer
reborn . . . and renewed.

PICK . . . UP . . . MY . . . CROSS

And follow Me!

Holy Dad

Satan, the great pretender,

mailed me a blender

hoping that I'd surrender

my heart;

that I'd plop it in

and watch it spin.

Instead, I licked the envelope,

clamped it,

pre-paid postage stamped it

and exit ramped it,

"Return to Sender".

My heart belongs to God

and you can't have it!

Ever since then, I've chased the snake, just like St. Patrick;

run the long race, allopatric;

with perfect faith, recite a tantric;

keep up the pace, break neck frantic;

trust in God, not in some lousy man trick.

This is a land of confusion,

where hands of intrusion

wield wands of illusion

and demands collusion

But like how a lighthouse can pierce through the murkiness

Jesus can cut through the quirkiness,

smooth over the jerkiness,

and draw out the perkiness.

"You've been given an invitation

to a world-wide celebration!"

declared the Holy Son

"The cheering will be so loud

that you'll be able to hear it

from coast-to-coast!"

"From Bagdad

and Carlsbad

to Leningrad

and Trinidad

there will be a huge party

with Holy Dad!"

Laugh Wild

Ashes to ashes
and chilled to a hush

Leave the child that's in my heart
Because You're asking for far too much

Footprints in the sand still are made of grains

And a coin may change nineteen hands
before it finds a home in yours.
Is the value then still the same?

Tell me -

        If you found life's meaning knockin' at your door

would you invite Him in - or not?

After all, the wound may not be fresh
and the congelation there be bitter,
but it is yours all the same.

I'n't it?

Self-reliance is a gift from Eden

       and

the crooked
     angel
had not a clue.

The Master Key

"I know the key
that is beyond my reach
is the one that can set me free.
I must have my freedom, so
guard, let me out!
Please let me have that key!"

"Why do you shout so?" was His reply.
"And why do you want that which cannot help you? The key
you want is merely a shadow and cannot gain you release.
The master key is right behind you on that shelf . . . within easy reach."

"Do you think me a fool?! Huh?! Would you have me believe
that it could be that easy? That you would put my freedom with me,
in the same room, behind locked iron bars?!
Why do you torment me so? Well,
I will not play a part in this game any longer.
You will have to look elsewhere for your amusement."

And with that he took the key and threw it out of the cell and
sent it clattering across the corridor floor.

The wizened old man, who was not really his guard, slowly
picked the key back up and placed it back on the shelf, again, within
easy reach.

"It will be there when you choose to use it." He said.
And under His breath He added, "If only this young fool
realized that this cell is of his own creation and the doorway is of Mine."

Mary

Mary had a little lamb
with fleece as white as snow
and wherever little Mary went
the lamb was sure to go.

Didn't you know little Mary,
that the world
slaughters
        lost lambs
for the sake of ninety-nine.

Perhaps your little one was wise
to stay so close to you
and perhaps there will be others
who will learn the same in time.

I surely do hope so,

for you see,

I'm a lost lamb too.

The Kiss of Judas

Judas kissed the Face of God
then betrayed Him for a price:

thirty silver pieces and his
                    eternal life

the potter's wheel
crushed the man who had abandoned God
while the potter's field mourned for its desecrated sod.

Learn not too late, young man, that everything has a price
and money is, indeed, important.

Work hard all your life,
make a living and do it well.

But that alone is not enough.

Offer unto God what you have wrought by your hand,
and your life as well.

Time

Tick Tock
goes the clock
Lady goes and gets botox.

Captain Hook,
his knees shook
thinking 'bout what time has took.

Tick Tock
goes the clock
inside the alligator.

He thought he could wait,
maybe deal with this later,

but time doesn't stop
even if you break the clock.
Someday, your heart will stop

Times like these, trust a savior
shock you with defribulator

then TIME will explode

and in Heaven ~ live forever!!

Mark

In High School I knew a kid named Mark. He had Cystic Fibrosis. In that condition, the oldest you can get is 17 or 18 years old, and most don't make it that far. I found out a long time ago that the best way to deal with people who are in that kind of situation is just to be honest, so I asked him point blank, "How does it feel knowing that you're probably not going to live as long as most other people?"

He just looked at me and said, "What? You gonna be jealous of a tree 'cuz it lives longer than you do? Hmmmph. What you got and for how long you got it for don't count for nuthin' in this world! The **only** thing that counts is what you do with what you got for the time that you've got it!"

Love

If you're lookin' for love
then you're lookin' in the wrong place.
You can't find love in a poem
and you'll never hear it
in the lyrics
of a song

Love ain't found in what you say;
it's only found in what you do.
Words can be used to express your love
but they can never be used to create it.

Now get out of here! I'm busy!

Cellar Door

Cellar Door
Effervescent Termination
Full-bodied Recrimination

Jesus Christ, Son of God
pieces heist, Icabob

Crane
Restrain, feign, shame

Linqua est acrior quam gladius
Hic discipulus
responsum clarius
dedit

Darnum, Darnum
whey ciatus
shaka ley, Fiatus
Biarno lay crayon matzo

What the hell am I talkin' about?
I don't know.

Bananas, kumquats and broccoli
roach motels and factories.

Dot to Dot Matrix
Oscar and Felix
Meyer and the Cat

Well, what about that?
The Cat and the Hat
Are you afraid of Green Eggs and Ham
I asked of Sam of Sam I Am

Plagiarism, esoteric

reggae, renew, renege

indecisiveness and precision
a very imprecise decision

Dangerously, Mattingly, eastwesterly

Jesus Christ, Son of God
pieces heist, Icabob

Cellar Door?
Cellar Door.

Mirror butt punt toe traffic
helium broadsword inclined trump zeppelin
Jericho rotation propulsion smith corona what for

eye propose
ewe compose
wheat carrion reflect zit
hook beat fart Barnum boot zoo

Elliot perception friendship excedrin
venetian polo blind current cliff better pool

walking
talking
basking
glory
glory
gory
glory

Every flower must bloom at it's own pace

If you try

      to pry

            the petals open

before it is it's time

Then you will have blood on your hands.

The glory of young women is their beauty

and the glory of young men is their strength

It is true that both are transitory

~ will not last for any length.

But do not burden them with thoughts of time borrowed

Is it not enough they enjoy the day?

There will be worries enough for them tomorrow

But for now, allow them to say,

"Good Morning."

Blood from Angels' Wings

Blood from angel's wings
pierced by roses thorns

Fallen petals adorned with grace

Your supple touch and gentle ways

Passionate embraces and love forsaken

Promises kept and broken

Love lost and never regained
rejoined by another, but never replaced

Christ's saving Hand and Mysterious Plan

Your soft amber hair and graceful posture

Thunderous applause and challenges not yet met

Nature's ways: both beautiful and savage

Secrets between friends, never betrayed-
not now, not ever

Successes, failures, disappointed and rejoice

Your intelligent eyes and lilting smile

Music that stirs the soul: Classical & Rock, Jazz & Blues

Obeying God's words, especially when it hurts

Adrenaline charging through my veins

And your friendship. God, yes, your friendship.

These are all a part of who I am. But I am not yet complete.

The Hermit & the Hoar

The Hermit and the Crucifix
buried in a hole - three days deep
and five wounds wide

Circumnavigated the berth of the globe
and pierced the bowels of the earth's
insides

The stone rolled away
and the hoar could see,
the Hermit no more
and the Crucifix free

Why do you search for the living among the dead?
Can you not see that He is not here?
Don't you remember what scriptures have said?

I am no longer a Hermit and you are no whore
This is a prayer answered and a promised renewed
Now let us dance with the Cross - the Cross so free

And drink deep
from the blood
of the Trinity.

The Seven Sacraments

From an obstetrician,

to a beautician,

to a mortician,

we entrust ourselves to professionals at every stage of life.

It's the same way with the church.

From baptism,

to first communion

to charism

and confirmation.

From Last rites

and funerals

to Columbus Knights

and priestly conferrals

we and God celebrate all of the wonderful milestones of life.

Why?

Because God loves a good party!

Blue Cross

If you wanta get the blues
You gotta pay your dues
but that doesn't mean you're covered.

If you've just got a bruise
they'll let you choose
from any number of over-priced doctors.
But if you need a high-priced procedure to stay alive
you'll blow a fuse
when you get the news
that the surgery ain't covered.

What does the insurance carrier have to be blue
about?
They're just a barker and a roustabout.
If we see a doctor, they'll clean us out.
And they have more medical clout
than the doctor ever will
as *they* decide which procedure we can or can't get
and decide how thick to pad our bill.

What do they have to be cross about?
They didn't find out
that their medical insurance is all maxed out
and you're reduced to begging for a frickin' hand-out
just to get a frickin' eye exam.
They never had to duke it out
with some pencil-necked medical school drop-out
who smiles at us blithely and ignores us

no matter how loud we shout.
And now we feel like we're the mark
in some grifter's flimflam scam.

Blue & Cross
Blue & Cross
A lot of us are feeling
mighty blue and
mighty cross.

P.S.A. 0.0

You are my God,

You are my tourniquet;

You are my surgeon

you are my scalpel cut.

You are my salvation;

my transfusion;

you are my radiation;

and my convalescence.

You are my chemo

without any side effects;

You are my diastolic and systolic;

you are the B.P. instruments.

You are my doctor's hand

and my nurses' guidance;

you are my promised land,

and my victory dance!

You are a P.S.A. of 0.0,

You are my Savior and rescued at-the-last-moment comic book hero.

Thank you, thank you, for saving my life!

Now take it, please, and graft it into the Tree of Life.

Paper Dragons

I long for simpler times-
of glory and of honor

When there were dragons to slay
and damsels in distress

But today's paper dragons
can't be swayed by sword nor armor

and women in power suits
need no heroes for their success

Family has no place and
there's no room for tradition

Instead they are supplanted
by power and by greed

So now we taunt the Dow Jones
with bankrupt suppositions

and we inflict greater wounds
and suffer injuries

So mock me if you must
and demote me to the jester

I have suffered worse and
know when I've been wronged

Diseases can flourish
when wounds are left to fester

When fools are made of men
who once were thought of strong.

Dance with God

Beautiful clouds that can't be seen
Beautiful stars in between

The night time
is the best time
to see the sky.

Constellations roll and bend
the abiding torrents have no end
in Jesus we have a noble friend

The best to fro and
the best behind
the greatest hills and knolls to climb

we over, between and just in time,
a wordless clown is just a mime.

a dirty soul that's unrefined
can still become pure over time

But only if that which was once alone
can become a palindrome.

Don't nod
Dogma, I am God.

We must to Heaven single file
all the women, men and child
all the spicy, tangy and mild
all the hellions so very wild

God is happiest when his children play
but it doesn't hurt for you to pray.
So please remember what I say:
It's best for you to learn today
that to dance with God in the fray
is the very, very bestest way
to dance and love and live and pray.

A Warrior King's Soliloquy

Am I worthy to lead?

There are many who think that I am.
And there are enough of those who follow.

But I know that this is a question that warrants strong consideration,
deserving of attention unencumbered by division,
so that the truth might be rendered slain upon the floor before us.

And I shall approach such a challenge with caution and with respect.

For I know that that very blood
which drips down the cross and into the flames of hell,
quenching for some and igniting for others . . .

That very blood which courses through the veins of the bowels of the earth . . .

That very blood, both innocent and pure, which was spilled upon the altar
for your redemption and for mine . . .

That very blood,   listens to my words now.

Am I worthy to lead?

There are times, I must confess, when I answer this question, with a resounding, "YES!"

And there are times when I feel that I am a God!

The weight of the wind of the world fills my skysails amidst the scatterings and the shatterings of a children's breeze.

And the star cables of my soul stretch out across the sky; constellation fragments are but thoughts for me. Synaptic chasms sputtering across the breadth of my soul.

While the brooding and plaintive flesh of the earth
        suck at granite feet,
planted like so many rows of corn and wheat.

The whole of the world is my throne and the gates of Hell my footstool.

Frightened child kid fear tidbits, combined with the fallen dreams of yesterage and the foolish pride of children pups forge together to form my scepter.

And the November morning hoar frost and the clattering jaws of blinking Irish girls-they be my blade.

Yes, there are times when I think that I am a God.

But then, there are other times, when I think, that I am not even . . .

a man.

But who then is to burden the blame of this upon my own, when I, among true others, must seek out my manhood in this new age world in which we live and fester, where we must bow and scrape so as never to offend.

A world in which we must pay for crimes never committed;
where we are held accountable for the sins of the past.
For the sins of fathers and father's fathers who came before us.

Beggar fools and warrior queens
Jester crowns and marish steeds
the worthiness of one
might be the pallor of another
and who among you is worthy to lead?

Come before me now-so I might knight thee.
For I know that I am not worthy of the honor.

There are two things, now, that I know certain of God:

1. YES!-there is a God. and
2. I ain't it.

So then,
perhaps I do not have unlimited power over all that I foresee,
But I wonder if I might be enough of a one to be a man?

I say that it is time for us to **be** men once again. Afraid not to embrace the hoards of the past, for if we must be imbued by the blight of their sins, then why not also benefit from their example?

Manhood-there was once a time when that word alone could inspire kings to rule and warriors to conquer. But today, the word spoken is enough to reduce the speaker to fool.

I know not why this is so.

We live in a world where there are no more rites of passage.
Where a boy no longer becomes a man through his first hunt, or his first battle.
And we have done nothing to fill the void.

Well,
I have pointed where we have been and where we are no longer.
Now, perhaps, it is for one mightier than myself to show the way from here.

But no mistake.

There is no stench as foul as a forgotten soul burning in a hell of his own creation.

And no scent as sweet as that same said man, resurrected from that heat, and guided back to the light from which he had been created in the first.

Three Short Days

Jonah and Lazarus and Jesus show us that you only need three days to change the world.

Jonah swallowed up by a Great White Shark;

three days in the stomach; three days in the dark,

He arrived in Nineveh, no worse for the wear, though he had partially digested clothes and slightly

singed hair.

But the most important thing to have changed was his heart, because, from the very start, he had

rebelled against God and he didn't care about the Assyrians.

But then he preached the word of God to them and then they were all saved, much to his chagrin.

And then that leads us to the New Testament and the story of Lazarus.

For three days in a tomb, his body already stiffening from rigor mortis

There was absolutely no doubt that he was completely dead

but then he rose from the grave

just by the power of what Jesus said.

Proof to everyone present and everyone who would come after

That Jesus has power over life and death and laughter.

Now we came to the three days in the tomb after Jesus' time on the cross

Proof again that he has the power to eliminate debits with credits and create new life from loss.

You would think Jonah was gobbled up and gone forever,

but it was the sailors who were abandoned and forever severed.

You'd think that Lazarus was dead and gone,

but it was the doubters who said shalom;

You'd think Jesus was just a victim of the justice system,

instead, it was the plotters who were justly condemned.

You'd think none of them would amount to anything,

but it was Pilate and Caiaphas who became enemies of the King.

The men who threw Jonah overboard;

Those who thought Lazarus was as stiff as a board

Those who plotted and conspired against my Lord

Thought they were victorious ~ for three days.

But then, three days later, the table was turned and one good turn deserves another

And each of these men *earned* their place in history

while the conspirators became footnotes in this sordid little story.

Corruption's victories are ugly and temporary ~ three days to be exact.

While resurrection's victories are infinite and celebratory ~ a real class act.

C'mon Satan, do your worst, 'cause you know Jesus will come up first!

If you think you're so clever as to destroy an innocent man's reputation

or throw an innocent man in prison

or get a guy fired just because you don't like him

Then enjoy your victory, while you may - because it's coming to an end . . . in three short days.

The Epistle of Paul
to the People of the City of Detroit

I, Paul, appointed by God the Almighty, and the submissive servant of the Eternal Lord Jesus Christ, the son of God, bring greetings to you, the peoples and magistrates of the city of Detroit within the great land of America.

Know that I have been watching you in spirit, and though it may seem that we are separated by vast distances and a chasm of centuries, know that I am forever with you and encourage you in our never-ending struggle to construct God's Kingdom here on Earth.

Detroit, least are you not among the great cities of the great country of America. If you believe that your automotive industry is unimportant within the workings of your society, then merely remind yourselves of the desperate isolation of those who do not have the benefit of such transportation. I shudder at the mere thought of what more could have been achieved in my lifetime if I had the use of but one of your automobiles.

But, while I am impressed by your many technological advances, I am equally in proportion aggrieved at your seeming abandonment of spiritual virtues. Yes Detroit, great has been your accomplishments and past generations salute you for your achievements. But now, at this point, it becomes necessary for me to point out what is painfully obvious to me and all other past generations, but what seems to elude your perceptions: there is a disease ravaging your community, and left unchecked, it will lead to your complete ruination and downfall. It is a disease of fear.

And what is fear but a lack of love.

Christ made the solution to this problem very simple, by expecting of us all but two simple commandments: Love your neighbor as yourself and love your Lord God with all your heart, mind, and soul.

And this brings us to the crux of this epistle. How is it Detroit, that against such a simple standard of measurement, you have failed so miserably? Detroit is the most racially segregated community in the United States; with the possible exceptions of Rio De Janeiro and South Africa, Detroit is the most racially segregated community on the face of the Earth! Your 8 Mile Road is a wall. The time has come to dismantle it.

As the walls of Jericho came crashing down with little more than the faith of those who marched around it, and as The Berlin Wall was crushed to splinters along with the Communist Rule that is came to represent, so too shall this wall come down as well. But make no mistake, as great as the moving of The Holy Spirit may have been throughout history, still nothing could have been achieved without the involvement of the people ~ and so shall this be expected of you.

There now exists within the inner city an overpowering sense of hopelessness and despair, and in the suburbs, one of apathy. These symptoms are merely opposite sides of the same coin, founded in the perverse belief that nothing can be done to improve the situation.

> Detroit is an abandoned city.
> Whites have abandoned Detroit.
> Successful blacks have abandoned Detroit.
> Big Business has abandoned Detroit.
> Banks have abandoned Detroit.

> Who is there left who has NOT left the city?!
> The answer? ~ God.
> God has not abandoned the City of Detroit.

He has heard the cries in the dark and He has answered those prayers. God cares not only for our spiritual needs, but for our physical and economic ones as well. Was not The Good Samaritan praised for healing the man's wounds, filling his belly and caring for his needs. Would you expect nothing less of God the Almighty? The church stands at the ready to fill the colossal gap left behind by the abandonment of this once great city that, *soon*, will be great again. And you need to be a part of that revival.

Seek out those who are already in leadership positions to save our city. Find out from them what you can do to help ~ and then do it! God smiles upon Focus: HOPE, which has become one of the top industrial producers for automotive and military technologies. Focus: HOPE employs over 500 people, and every one of the industrial engineers who works there were once homeless or on welfare.

This is only one example. Seek out those who are making a difference within your city and then do what you can to help. Once progress is made and maintained, others will follow the example. And then . . . the inexplicable tension that now exists between city and suburbs will be lessened; the suffocating grip that poverty now has over the city will be loosened; and, of course, the inevitable crime rate that always accompanies impoverished areas will be reduced also. All that is required is the willingness to do the work and the proper leadership. If it is truly God's will, then The Holy Spirit will manifest Itself and bring together all the people needed to complete the task.

But understand Detroit that we are not fighting merely for the sake of one city. Remember the riots in Los Angeles that was so hauntingly reminiscent to the Detroit riots of 1968.

And don't forget the more recent events of New Orleans: a mighty city that was first struck down by a natural disaster, and then struck down again, by those fleeing the city and unwilling to help those who were poor and did not have the money to travel; left to be drowned in an atmosphere of "Well, better them than me." ha ha ha.

My suspicions have been confirmed that the rest of the country is destined to suffer Detroit's fate, if something is not done soon. But I firmly believe that you can achieve what others deem as impossible and Detroit can become a model city which the rest of the nation can turn to as an example.

You now know the task that lies before you.

I implore you, brothers and sisters of Christ, be on your guard against anybody who encourages trouble or who would scatter obstacles before you. Avoid them. They are slaves of their own appetites, confusing the simple-minded with their pious and persuasive arguments. But I have faith in your ability to discern the truth.

May the God of Peace make you perfect and holy. God has called you and He will not fail to strengthen you for the task. May the Grace of our Lord Jesus Christ be with you always.

And I am forever your humble servant, Paul of Tarsus.

I'm celibate!

I'm celibate!

I'm not doing it for the hell of it.

I'm spiritually strong because I'm sexually pure

You don't believe me?

Let me give you a tour.

I keep my junk in my pants

so I don't have to take a chance

on the rubber breaking

or she is faking

and I'm not taking

someone's virginity.

You don't think that's worth something?

Not playing with your ding-a-ling?

A sexual tryst ain't worth anything

to our Lord and Savior Christ the King.

If you're promiscuous then you're a weakling!

I'm trying to become a heavenly star

but if you can't manage to go that far

then you better believe that I'm stronger than you are.

I'm celibate!

I'm celibate!

I'm not doing it for the hell of it.

The Stain

There are cigarette stains
on my upper lip
and they will never wash away

I see black rain
falling from a sky
with no clouds

And still, it calls my name

Held betwixt two fingers,
still it holds me in it's grip.
It wears a wall of mist
as it's shroud.

It tempts me with a fragrance
as sweet as Honeysuckle Rose
Then takes away my breath
with twenty bare-knuckled blows

And still, I crave the stain.

Economics 101

GENIUS is the capacity to see what is not there.

INDUSTRY is wanting to fill that hole up.

CAPITALISM is building a mountain where that hole used to be.

GREED is selling off pieces of the mountain to the highest bidder.

And the *FOOL* is the one who nabs the biggest piece from the
bottom of the mountain, and sends the whole damn thing tumbling down,

until finally, some genius comes along and says, "Hey, that's a hole!"

Return to Sender

I don't have time to be philosophical anymore-
I've got too many bills to pay.

Don't look to me for the answers anymore.
I don't even know how an ipod works.

I am not poetic
Only my writing is

Yet people still turn to me
because I write poetry.

Don't you people get it?
I'm just askin' the questions.

The rest is up to you.

The Thomas B. Finan Center

The Thomas B. Finan Center
a place spent in hibernating winter
the staff are like the three bears snoring
and the patients are like Goldilocks exploring.

Searching for a vein of truth
wasted youth; so uncouth
Clark Kent in a telephone booth

And our subject today is: How to fly.

Red Bull may give you wings
but there's another in-between;
Tinker Bell may have pixie dust
but sooner or later it turns to rust;
you may have fun on a hang glider
but I know someone who can take you higher;
and there may be a mission to Mars
but that's not really all that far;
you may feel free on a bungee jump cord
but you're better off to trust the Lord ~

He will teach you how to soar!

One if by land and two if by sea
and our next lesson is aqua-marine
and we all live in a yellow submarine,
a yellow submarine,
a yellow submarine,

and last night I had the strangest dream
that I was doing battle with leviathan and some squid
and God stood like a referee
between the ego and that slippery li'l id.

whether we're a cosmonaut
or a deep sea diver
we still need to be
a mountain climber

Because there are mountains to be climbed
no matter where we go.

There are mountains on distant planets
There are mountains deep under the sea
There are mountains within each other
There are mountains in you and me.

The inner realm is greater in landscape
and more powerful in dimension
than the outer realm ever was

There are people here who want to help us
our own personal Tibetan Sherpas

with the staff, the patients & God united,
the sick are healed, the blind are sighted.

And remember,

you do not conquer the mountain,
you become one with it,
and then you reach the sky ~ together.

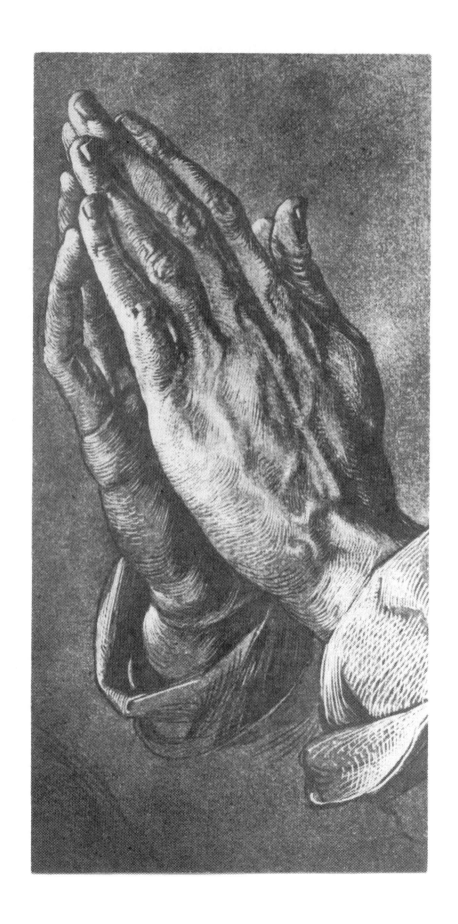

A Prayer

Today I swear to do the best I can.
Help me with the rest, Oh Lord.

Where I am weak, strengthen me.

Where I am lost, guide me.

Where I am proud, humble me.

Where I am foolish in the ways of men,
Teach me the wisdom of the Lord.

Where I am selfish, teach me altruism.

Where I am greedy, teach me charity.

Where I am thoughtless, teach me respect.

Where I am self-indulgent, teach me sacrifice.

And where I am doubtful of the Word of God,
Teach me the power of prayer.

Thank You, God, for being there for me.
Thank You for Your strength, beauty,
power and love.
I still don't understand why You've decided to
be my God. But I love You for it.

I love You.

The Summer of '91

The Teenage Mutant Ninja Turtles
   BeBop and Rock Steady

We've fallen and we can't get up!
   Oh get up and get on with your lives already!

William Blake and the Doors
   Jim Morrison and Windex

Moving fast in tight pants
   Dacron and Spandex

What's wrong with this picture?
Is the screen getting blurred
or is the horizontal out of whack?
Is there something wrong with me
or is the whole world suffering
a Big Mac Attack?

Why did they mess with Classic Coke?
and
Have you heard any good jokes lately?

You got sex on your mind
you could get arrested
or lose your job,
like Pee Wee.

What's wrong with this picture?
Is the screen getting blurred
or is the horizontal out of whack?
Someone pinch me before I go blind
Oh ~ never mind ~
I'll just have myself a snack.

KACHING!

The Cat in the Hat

I am the cat in the hat Tom,

I am the cat in the hat.

I cause things to sway

and cause disarray

I am the cat in the hat.

You ask Me to leave,

because you believe

I'll cause something to break or to stumble

I am the redeemer

you are the receiver

all that's required: Don't grumble!

I unblock occlusions

I am the solution

and I cause everything to end in a wonderful conclusion

and what's wrong with that?

Don't tell me to scat

I am the cat in the hat!!!

Battle Rap

Words are power
words can empower
and cleanse like a shower.

But now all of you want me to cut into this man here.

I know how powerful words are.
They can cut; they can destroy.

This ain't no game; he ain't no toy.
I can't tear off his arms and then glue them back.
this ain't no death trap Big Mac attack.

You can't take back the words once you've said them.
You can't take back crossing that line once you've tread them.

Words can show vision; words can inspire.
But you want derision and senseless hate fire.

I can give you beautiful and majestic words
but all you want is shit talkin' cuss turds.

You got a handful of human feces
but you think its Reese's Pieces
and you chow down.

You're that stupid fool
who found the Baby Ruth
in the swimming pool
in that movie Caddy Shack.

Knick Knack Paddy Whack
give the dog a bone

Chompin' on a stool
that you found in the pool
and now he thinks he's cool.

But now bad breath man
can't figure out why he's all alone.

Luther Campbell strings together
a line of curse words
and now he thinks he's a genius.

A genius? He's not even
a rap poetry fetus.

Luther Campbell of 2 Live Crew
talkin' trash and thinkin' from his penis.
Is that the best he can do?

Beltin' out "Banned in the U.S.A."
and preachin' it like he's Martin Luther King
what the hell's he's tryin' to say?
that he can't rap unless he talks trash
and everyone knows he can't sing.

Don't you have nuthin' better to do
than to prove to God
that you ain't got nuthin' better in you?

Do you care more about a hip-hop doggie-drop skank-weed rag-talk
than about the truth?!
Trash-tv fast-track libidinous jerkin-off Jerry Springer wanna-bes, who do not breath
poetry.

There **_IS_** sumthin' better in you. There is poetry in you.

Christ used words
They flew like birds
They penetrated people's hearts
and took them back to the start
like new-born babes.
Words can bring you back
to God's well-laid

plans
stand
clan

God's hand
Promised land.

You gotta answer that bugle call

One is from Satan,
the other's from God.

And which one you give the nod
is gonna decide
whether you fly
or whether you fall.

American Idol

We do not have admiration
for that particular train station

American Idol is about the fame train
we're talkin' about the prophet rocket

one is earth bound, the other is not.

What do you think we're tryin' to say?

sock it to me?
rock it to me?
rock tyranny?
explosive energy
       and nowhere to go but gone
       and yesterday's news.

The bad news bears
and who cares anyway

And now we're talkin' bout Fantasia

ooohhh, she's a sure bet
a triple threat
on a cripple's quest

Tryin' to make it on the nod of the judges
and she's hopin' that God don't hold grudges
when you dance on the sod it smudges
and now here's God givin' her some nudges . . .

. . . for her to go in the right direction
so she can pass a holy inspection
but now there's just one more question ~

will she go where God shows?

Don't worry, I'll agree to go away
if you agree to change your name.

Don't you know that God don't like no false idols?

55

I Broke some Eggs Today

I broke some eggs today.
There they were-spluttering and splattering in the pan,
those twin yellow-orange eyes staring up at the ceiling
through a thin white slice of bubbling cloud that was just
beginning to crisp at the edges. Just the way I like it.

But,
when I went to transfer the eggs from skillet to plate, the
handle broke and the pan went clattering to the floor.
When I picked it back up, there was revealed a children's
finger painting swirling on the floor.

I picked the splattered eggs up with a spatula,
put them on a plate,
and ate them anyway.

I used pepper to camouflage the little specks of dirt that I
saw floating around in the egg whites and yolks,
But I could use nothing to cover the shame I knew was
spreading across my face.

But,   I didn't go hungry today

Nope.   Not today.

History

First you see it,
then you forget it,
then you remember it,
and then you live it!

But then,

it's too late.

DASH

Watcha gonna do with your dash?

You know, like on a tombstone.

There's the year you were born.

There's the year you die.

And there's a dash in between.

That dash is your life.

Watcha gonna do with your dash?

Big Words

People who use big words really get my goat;

they want to shove it down your esophagus instead of down your throat.

Instead of talking about their environment, they use a word like milieu.

Instead of talking about a sneak attack they say that it was a coup.

A big word doesn't have to be that long;

instead of saying syllable, they mouth a word like diphthong.

They say Jesus was buried in a sarcophagus instead of in a grave

and they say that He extricated instead of that He saved.

What's the big idea of using big words? I think they stink like onions.

Try being pithy instead of being sesquipedalian.

I think Abraham Lincoln said it best,

"Know all the big words but use only the small ones."

A PICTURE PAINTS A THOUSAND WORDS

BUT THERE ARE CERTAIN WORDS THAT CAN CONVEY

WHAT A THOUSAND PICTURES CANNOT SAY

The Apology

I looked into your dark eyes
But all that I could see
was deep youthful challenge
but throughout it all-no pretense.

Now I look within my own archives
perhaps to find some remedy
But for me to gain redemption
will take more
than mere repentance.

Though that would be a good start.

Although I did not mean to do so,
I took advantage of your trust
and my pen strayed where it had no place.
For me to make demands now would be blasphemy

I have no right to say
you should or that you must
But since a day cannot go by
when you cannot see my face
I will take the risk and **ask** you,
"Please forgive me."

And I mean that from the heart.

There was a Child Went Forth

There was a child went forth everyday;

And the first object he looked upon, that object he became;

And that object became a part of him for the day, or a certain part of the day, or for many years, or stretching cycles of years.

As he left the house he could immediately see his breath on the frigid winter air, like he were seeing through the eyes of a slumbering dragon, and he could hear the crunch of the snow beneath his feet.

He saw a snowman sweating in the hot afternoon sun, but still striking a confident pose.

Boys pelted each other in a snowball fight, hiding behind snow forts that they had built, while an older girl, trotting up a staircase, clutched at her blown skirt.

Old Mr. Quinn shoveled his driveway, with his winter coat unzipped, because of how warm it had become.

The child could see Christmas trees through hoarfrost covered window panes and holiday decorations adorning people's homes while, in one house, a menorah blazed defiantly.

He stopped to gawk at the tacky Vanderbilt home, who always went overboard with the life-sized Santa, sled and reindeer on the roof and the animatronic snow people on the lawn.

He heard carolers down the street, entertaining people at their front doors.

Just then, it started to snow again, lightly, at first, but gaining speed. He looks behind to see his footprints disappear and the puddles start to freeze.

A plow truck scraped along the roadway, deflecting snow to the curb.

Always . . . always . . . when you go to bed at night and everything is brown and green, and you wake up in the morning, and everything is white, there's something magical about that. Of course, a little bit goes a long way and, after months of trudging through the snow and shoveling the snow, it gets old pretty quick, and everyone is grateful for the coming of spring.

But still, the beauty of the changing seasons became a part of that child who went forth everyday, and who now goes, and will always go forth everyday.

~ Based on the summertime imagery in Walt Whitman's poem, "There was a Child Went Forth".

Ridiculous Miraculous

Be willing to be ridiculous so that, through you, the Lord can be miraculous.

As you matriculate and educate don't hesitate or overcomplicate as you learn this important lesson:

If you're willing to have fun, then you'll be able to do what others say cannot be done.

It's not enough to just go to mass on weekends and read the good book.

You gotta get in the game!

What a shameif

you're totally lame

and you're content to just sit on the bench and do nuthin' but look.

Life is not a spectator sport!

It's for the athletic sort

who plays and has fun on the backcourt.

Be willing to be ridiculous so that, through you, the Lord can be miraculous.

If you're so worried about how you look

and you're overly dignified

then you'll just end up a schnook at the retirement home

who never really tried.

Be willing to act like a little boy;

be willing to act like a little girl

so you can partake in the joy

of trying to make this a better world.

Then you'll be foolish enough to make a difference;

then you'll be a person of consequence;

then you'll be a person of confidence

and of gold and myrrh and frankincense.

Be willing to be ridiculous so that, through you, the Lord can be miraculous.

What some people see as impossible

we just see as a three-point shot and a double-dribble.

If you stop being so serious

you can become goofy and delirious

and then you can turn the whole thing into a game,

and then you can exclaim,

"What a victory we got in God's Name!"

and then you can enter the Kingdom of Heaven Hall of Fame!

What others will see as a coincidence

you'll know is God's astronomical providence,

all made possible because you were willing to be ridiculous

and because you and God were on the same dream team,

you'll be redeemed by the Holy Spirit regime

and, together, you will achieve the miraculous!

and that ain't no pipe dream!

(Pictured above from left to right: Elizabeth Bederka, Kathleen Paonessa Trastevere, Tom Paonessa, Mike Paonessa, Teresa Paonessa Bederka, Carol O'Malley.)

Family Portrait

There were two little boys and two little girls

each of us living in our own little worlds.

Teri learned languages and Kathy played the guitar;

perhaps these hobbies didn't take them far,

but it prepared them for a wonderful life,

filled with both happiness and with strife

one became a chemist, the other a soldier.

They both raised families as they grew a little older.

Tom and Mike were in a different world altogether;

such is life for a couple of fraternal twin brothers.

They were as different as different could be;

one was John Belushi, the other Fred's pal, Barney.

They went to a boarding school together and hung out with the guys.

Neither one of them was much of a prize.

Mike wanted to be an inventor, Tom a writer.

The boys followed their dreams, one as an author, the other a designer.

Neither one of us raised a family. For Mike, it was his biggest regret.

For Tom, who became a monk, he considered it to be his biggest asset.

But before we even got started, while we were still little kids,

Dad, who smoked five packs a day, faced the consequences for what he did.

He got cancer, all up in his lungs, and he became very angry, and that was very hard on his daughters and sons.

He didn't give us a very heroic example.

When we looked to him for guidance, we instead get trampled.

When he died, we cried, but it was also a relief.

Let's face it, he had been as distant as the Great Barrier Reef.

Perhaps because her male role model wasn't very strong,

Teri would go out with the first guys who came along.

Because of her bad choices, life for Teri was very hard,

she had to admit that the guy she married was a big blowhard.

Teri was jealous of Kathy in her choice of a mate.

She remembered George, who treated her better,

instead she got branded with a scarlet letter

and she knew in her heart that it was too late.

The only good thing to come from that union

was the heaven-sent blessing of four wonderful children.

Teri and Kathy, the two little girls,

loved each other in their own little world.

Tom and Mike were in their own little clique.

It went on this way until Teri got sick.

She got breast cancer that migrated to her brain.

It was like dealing with Dad all over again.

She was as angry and as resentful as Dad.

I was with her at the Grand Canyon ~ it was real bad.

But the last conversation that we ever spoke was about Grandpa and his fishing boat,

and that was the inspiration for the novel I wrote.

I'm sad that the writing of that book is now finally over.

Every time I put pen to paper was a new story and another adventure.

I felt that Teri was with me every day that I wrote it.

She became an integral part in my becoming a poet.

Then came the death of our mother and brother,

each of them dying within ten days of each other.

I can't tell you what a tragedy it is to lose a twin.

I cried every day for six months and if I think about it much, it starts all over again.

Mike and I were together in the womb;

I remember when mom and dad used a sheet to bisect our room;

and we used it as an excuse to play peek-a-boo.

He was my best friend, always and forever.

That is still true, even though we're no longer together.

And, of course, mom was the glue that held our family together.

She was a Doctor of Education and worked in administration

Losing her was like a tether ball losing its tether.

So now, Kathy's partner in crime is now gone

and Tom's brother waved goodbye and said, "So long."

So now, Kathy's little girl world is now half-erased

and Tom's little boy world has done an about face

and, whether we care to admit it or not,

you and I, kid, are all that we got.

So, now our two worlds have collided

and the two of us together have decided

that, like it or not, you and I are all that we have left.

Do not cry; do not be bereft, for we still have each other ~

a little girl and a little boy sister and brother.

I love you, Kathy.

Vivamus mea Lesbia, atque amamus,
rumoresque senum seueriorum
omnis unius aestimemus assis!

Let us live, my Lesbia, and let us love
and let us care not for the chitterings
and chattering of others
for they are but jealous of the love that
we have for each other!

The Soliloquy of Cattullus

Lesbia, sweet Lesbia,

we may live
and we may love

but we shall do so on our own.

And we may have no more grievance
than our tragic loss of time

and I'll forgive you your transgressions
if you'll forgive me mine.

But still,
we shall be in two different places
when we speak of home.

And we may live
and we may love

but we shall do so . . . on . . . our . . . own.

The Voyage

I had a dream
but all that's left
is what I thought
was once adrift

but now I discover
a truth
that's undercover:

That only the stories are true.

Batten hatches; hold on fast!
Hold onto the ship's main mast
yell out to all the swimmers,
better climb out of the river

"find something to hold onto
a piece of driftwood will not do
better climb aboard the boat
good intentions do not float!"

The waves get really high
someone screams, "We all gonna die!"

Thoughts of death seize us
nothing can aleve us
this is so egregious!
Do our eyes deceive us?
Or is that Jesus
walking on the waves.

Can this be true?

All is well, we're all saved
This won't be our watery grave
No sirree, not today.

But Jesus, He just looks at us
He seems a little bit depressed
And He didn't seem to have very much to say.

"I have power over land and water
but I don't hear their joy and laughter
until I'm in the midst of them.
Don't they know how much they matter?
Don't they know they're my sons and daughters?

And I would never leave them in the fray!"

And He cares that much for you too!

So put aside our differences
embrace our different universes;
it doesn't matter if your slovenly
you can still be heavenly;
and do an about-face
as He tries to erase
all of the mistakes
that come between God and you.

You can feel so elated
as you your spirit is inflated
and you trade in your ego for a soul.
Don't worry if you're eviscerated
God never hesitated
to heal whatever complicated
you as we all row.

We're in the boat together
we can float whatever weather
so long as we stay tethered
to the Lord!

God's favorite word is collaborate
He loves to sail as we celebrate
on a journey that He navigates

There's no reason to fear any Jolly Roger pirates
if God had surrendered to a thousand Pontius Pilates
He still would have risen from the grave.

At the end of our long voyage
is some hot cocoa and some porridge
and a mother's loving glance
as we slurp from the glass.

Our raincoats and galoshes
used for puddle jumps and sloshes
have been hung up with care to dry.

They've been put there by our mother
she put them next to our brother's
side by side.

That's my brother ~ little boy Jesus
He wipes his nose with his sleeve and sneezes
then he asks his mom for some macaroni and cheeses.

What's a mother to do?

Through the spirit of adoption
we've been given the clear option
to put an end to sibling rivalry

Jesus is our brother
and Mary is our mother
and together we're one big happy, holy family

Want to be adopted too?

I awoke from my dream
but things did not seem
to be as they had been once before.

The world was just the same
nothing else had been changed
it was only myself who had in tempest, forged:

a new heart, where fear could find no lodging
a spirit redeemed by a thorny-crowned God-King
and a playfulness, like a goose-down gosling.

And then I knew:

You never can grow old, if your spirit is anew.

There's a feast up in Heaven
they'll be pizzas and bran muffins
reases' pieces and easy-bake ovens
and ever so much more

so won't you please try to join us
as we need you in the chorus
we're waiting for you on Heaven's shore.

Please don't deprive us.

Don't make us go on
in a Heaven without you.

The Fear of Angels

Angels fear to tread
where men live day by day

And truly can you blame them?

For if men only knew
what peril
their souls were in
from what they say
and how they say it
and from those deeds
that are measured
cross that line
they call
their lives,

then, truly, then
they too would fear
before the evening's end.

The Holy Spirit

Are you filled with The Holy Spirit?

C'mon now, let me hear it!

We need a Catholic Charismatic Renewal,

and then we'll have the Best of Both Worlds:

both the blessed sacraments and The Holy Spirit unfurled!

We need the Church, but we need The Holy Ghost, too.

Preach it!

Teach it!

and The Holy Eucharist, too!

Let's get filled with The Holy Spirit!

C'mon now, let me hear it!

Most Catholics are a reserved bunch

who think that Speaking in Tongues is a bunch of junk.

They look at them like they're mentally ill,

but they never lived their lives following God's Will.

Are you filled with The Holy Spirit?

C'mon, show it!

C'mon, sow it!

C'mon, row it!

C'mon, tow it!

C'mon, get filled with The Holy Spirit!

Fill it!!!

Fashion Sense Nonsense

Capri pants and a pair of jeans
walking down the street
and a couple of women inside of them
trying not to preen.

Hospital scrubs
with Winnie-the-Pooh figurines,
pockets laden with goodies ~ a coke and a candy bar ~
and a stethoscope in-between.

Jethro style overalls
and work-men's clothes with
work-men's boots and
work-men's gloves
surrounding a work-man,
who at the moment is ill-disposed,
waiting for his turn
to churn the concrete
with the jack-hammer.

A mini-skirt and flouncy blouse,
high-heels tap-tapping on the marble-like slate of the linoleum floor.
Perhaps a tawdry girl, looking for a chance to flirt and joust
with the next bedlam stranger.
But she is hanging on the sleeve of a tousled shirt atop a midriff belt
and come-hither trousers, her date inside of them,
alerting all others that these clothes are for each other and no one else.

A frumpy girl in work-out sweats and sensible underwear underneath.
A guy walking in the opposite direction, not dressed to impress, goin' commando.

All of humanity on parade
amidst the smell of aftershave.

A red dress with a high bodice, snug just beneath the swollen breasts and
the tailored canopy to make way for the swollen belly;
the pregnant women desperate to downplay the changes that have taken place in her body
but also, announce them to the world.

Panama shorts reveal a Don-Joy knee-brace, strapped snugly around the leg of an old man
with ACL troubles and leaning heavily on his cane.

Pajama bottoms walking around, unashamed, worn by a woman who doesn't mind wearing such attire even in public.
Of course men could never get away with that because, without a purse, they carry everything around in their pockets, and pajamas never have enough of those.

FUBU attire clothe a young black guy walking on by ~ a sad misnomer.
FOR US ~ BY US.
And yet, hand-tailored by cheap Mexican labor and
distributed by the powerful elite, who are almost certainly white.

Flip-Flops clopping;
baby-strollers strolling;
Western boots clomping along, but almost certainly not a cowboy;
basketball shoes two sizes too big and laces left untied.
Nike ~ the Greek goddess of Athletic competition.
Puma ~ a wild cat ready to pounce.
& Air Jordan's ~ a shoe that never promises that you'll jump as high as the person for whom they're named.

Tank-tops, halter-top mini-skirts with polka dots, draped over matching slacks and stiletto heels with straps that wrap around the ankle and calf, like the Ancient Romans,
but inside a teenage girl, flaunting bravado and betraying indecisiveness
at the same time.

Corn-rows with beads atop pastel-colored short-sleeves
and shorts to match, a little girl and her mother out for a walk.

Hip-hugger jeans ~ I've never liked those.
I've never been a big fan of muffin-tops and whale-tails
and certainly not butt-cracks.
And the obligatory lower back tattoo, looking like a bat in flight.

All of humanity on parade amidst the smell of aftershave.

They say clothes makes the man
but what I don't understand
is that I always feel just the same.

Joan River's obnoxious question of "Who are you wearing?" is lost on me.

Fashion is nice
and it can fetch quite a price

but it has no connection to eternity.

Blood from Angel's Wings

Blood from Angel's Wings
pierced by roses thorns

and a guitar with a broken string
still can sing a sweet and wounded tune

And the percussionist, after
he thumped out his long back tones
with his callous covered hands,

smiled,

and said,

> "Hay rides and lonely souls
> candy canes and suicide
> final bows are part of the show
> but life goes on, even when life is over.

God has promised to make Easter lovers of us all.

But . . . you gotta believe."

And with that,

                    He spread his wings
                           and
                      tried to fly.

YOU GOTTA BELIEVE!